P9-CET-068

BASKET

Copyright © 1994 Jean Wells

Edited by Barbara Konzak Kuhn

Technical information edited by
Joyce Engels Lytle

Cover and book design by Morris Design,
Monterey, California

Electronic illustrations by Ginny Coull

Photography by Ross Chandler, Bend, Oregon

The author wishes to thank Ursula Searles,
for quilt making and inspiration.

The author also thanks VIP Fabrics,
Fabric Traditions, and Fairfield Processing
Corporation for assistance with materials.

ISBN 0-914881-74-4

Published by C&T Publishing
P.O. Box 1456, Lafayette, California 94549

Printed in Hong Kong

Books by Jean Wells

Fans

A Celebration of Hearts
(with Marina Anderson)

Picture This
(with Marina Anderson)

Memorabilia Quilting

Patchwork Quilts Made Easy Series:
The Basket Quilt
The Bear's Paw Quilt
The Country Bunny Quilt
The Milky Way Quilt
The Nine-Patch Quilt
The Pinwheel Quilt
The Sawtooth Star Quilt
The Stars & Hearts Quilt

No-Sew Appliqué Series:
Bloomin' Creations
Fans, Hearts, and Folk Art
Holiday Magic
Hometown

For a complete listing of fine quilting books
from C&T Publishing, write to:
C&T Publishing, P.O. Box 1456,
Lafayette, CA 94549

Welcome to *The Basket Quilt* beginning quilt book. You will find a large variety of basket ideas and quilt projects with many different themes. There are Victorian-style baskets embellishing simple pillows, a *Lancaster Medallion* quilt, plus an *Old-Fashioned Basket* quilt with the baskets set on their sides. For easy construction, the simple basket shape is drafted with a pieced handle that eliminates the necessity for appliqué.

The easy, recipe-style instructions and graphics are "quilter friendly." They lead you through the quilt making process, making it fun. By following the quick-cutting instructions and using a rotary cutter, plastic ruler, and mat, the cutting will be fast and accurate.

Approach your quilting project as a student, using the book as your guide, or pretend you are in my classroom! I have been a quilting instructor for twenty-three years and my beginners' classes are still my very favorite to teach. Read all of the general instructions before you begin. I want your quiltmaking experience to be a successful one.

Creating a new quilt is exciting and learning is easy with the *Patchwork Quilts Made Easy* series.

About the Author

Jean Wells' fascination with fabrics and stitching started in childhood and culminated in The Stitchin' Post, a successful retail store, which she founded eighteen years ago in the small mountain community of Sisters, Oregon.

Jean teaches quiltmaking on a national level as well as in her store. She shares ideas through quilting books for C&T Publishing, leaflets for Leisure Arts, magazine articles, and free-lance design work for Offray Ribbons, McCall's Patterns, and Fabric Traditions. Her personal approach continues to captivate her readers, her students, and her customers.

GETTING STARTED

What is a Quilt?

A quilt contains three layers, like a sandwich with a fancy top. The top can be patchwork (smaller pieces of different fabrics sewn together) or it might be appliqué (the application of a shape onto a surface); or, it might be a combination of both. The middle layer is batting—a non-woven filler material usually made of polyester and sometimes of cotton. The backing is a layer of fabric under the batting. Quilting is the process of stitching the three layers together so the batting doesn't move around. It may be done by hand or by sewing machine.

How do you choose fabric?

Choosing 100% cotton fabrics will make your job easier. Cotton is more flexible and has a soft, comfortable hand. It takes a press well. Use fabrics that are tightly woven and of the same weight. A broadcloth weight is most commonly used in quiltmaking.

Selecting your fabric is a very individual experience. Most people have the ability to choose successfully if they just think about the relationships in the quilt block. The basket block is simple. There is the basket and the background that it sits in. If there are strips of fabric between the blocks these are called sashing. Think of the fabrics in the quilt as friends. They need to have something in common, but they should also stand on their own as individuals.

Pre-wash all fabrics. Some will shrink a small amount and the darker colors may run. I pre-wash just as I would wash the finished project.

The Mood of the Quilt

Think about the theme of the quilt. Where will it be used, or who is it for? What kind of mood will it project? This is the fun part of quilting—searching for fabrics that reflect the theme.

Look at *Basket Trellis* on page 12. The background fabric is the same in all the blocks, but from one large print. When cutting smaller pieces from fabric with a larger design, no two are alike. This adds visual interest. The individual basket fabrics are an array of different floral prints on black backgrounds. The striped fabric between the blocks helps to break up and define the floral feeling. Try combining different styles of fabric like florals and stripes.

The Lancaster Medallion on page 14 consists of three colors: black, red and turquoise. I like the dramatic effect of bright colors placed against black. Looking at the use of color in pictures of Amish quilts was my inspiration for this quilt.

Old-Fashioned Baskets on page 16 is just that, old-fashioned. Several years ago I saw a quilt in a museum that had baskets set on their sides facing each other. Finding colored fabrics with a "mellow mood" and setting them on a deep tan background re-created the feeling and look of the antique quilt.

Get in the habit of observing. Look at a quilt and evaluate what it is that you like about it. Is it the colors, the arrangement of the blocks, or the border design that draws your attention? Think about it objectively, then store this analysis away in your memory. You will draw on this knowledge later in your quiltmaking.

Value and Contrast

When you have selected two fabrics that you think might work in the basket block, put them beside each other and walk away. Turn around and glance at them just for a moment. The impression you get is a lasting one. If there is not enough contrast, the basket will fade into the background and you will loose the image. This is contrast: the difference between light and dark. If the two colors blend together, they are too close in value. Value is the degree of lightness or darkness in a color. You need contrast in quilting fabrics. Go back and change one of the fabrics to a lighter or darker version.

Another way to check contrast is to photocopy the fabrics. The copy machine reduces your colored fabrics to black and white, showing you the contrast.

Add sparkle to your quilt with small amounts of lighter, darker, or brighter fabrics. In *Old-Fashioned Baskets* it is the dark burgundy in the border that serves this function, while in *Lancaster Medallion* it is the use of the turquoise with the red and black. This touch of color makes the other colors work better, and your quilt will be livelier.

What tools are needed?

❖ **Rotary cutter**—A round, very sharp blade is mounted on a plastic handle. It looks like a pizza cutter. I like the larger cutter.

❖ **Cutting mat**—This is made of plastic and comes in various sizes. It protects the table during cutting. The 18" x 24" size is ample.

❖ **Cutting ruler**—This ⅛"-thick plastic ruler is designed for quilters. It is marked in 1", ½", ¼", and ⅛" increments. A 6" x 12" ruler is fine for the projects in this book.

❖ **Fabric shears**—sharp fabric-cutting scissors

❖ **Straight pins**—Quilters prefer the longer, glass-headed pins.

❖ Paper scissors
❖ Seam ripper
❖ Tape measure
❖ Iron
❖ **Sewing machine**—Make sure it is in good working order.
❖ **Sewing thread**—A cotton thread is best when you work with cotton fabrics. Match the thread to the basic mood of the quilt. For most quilts, I use a dull tan. If the quilt is very dark or light, then change the thread color. When machine quilting, find a bobbin thread that matches the back of the quilt.
❖ **Monofilament thread**—This looks like a clear, thin fishing line. It is often called invisible thread. It is used in the top of your machine when machine quilting.

Quilting Tools

❖ **Medium-size safety pins**—(*Optional*) they may be used for basting the quilt layers together.
❖ **⅝"-wide masking tape**—This is used in quilt basting.
❖ **¼" masking tape**—This is used to mark quilting lines for hand quilting.
❖ **Quilting needles**—Sizes 8 to 10 Betweens are good for hand quilting.
❖ **Quilting hoop**—A 14" to 18" hoop is used for hand quilting.
❖ **Marking tools**—A fine, hard lead pencil (0.5) will wash out, as will a silver pencil. Always check washability first!

Four Basket Pillow

Basket Trellis

Single Basket Pillow

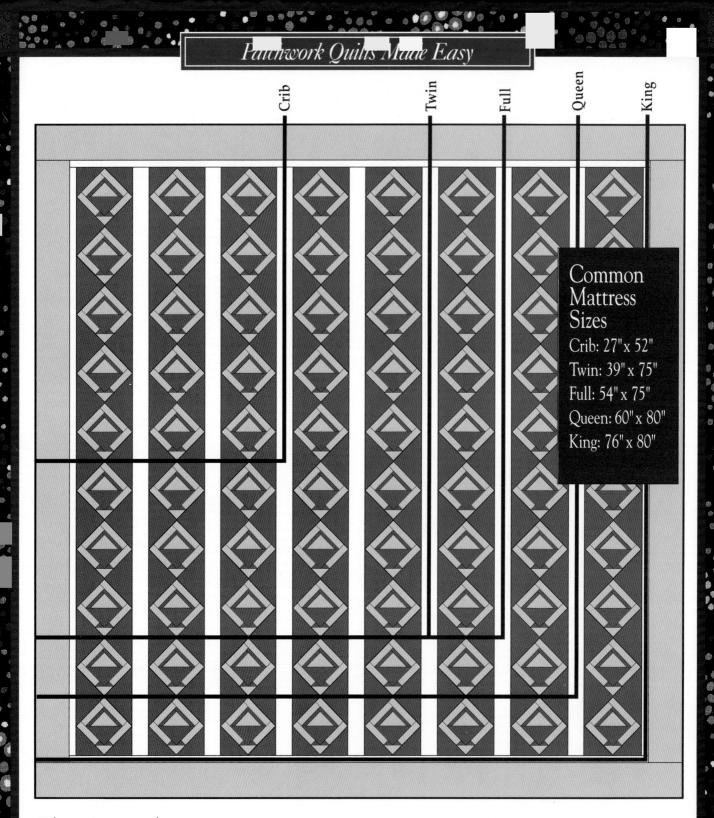

Crib | Twin | Full | Queen | King

Common Mattress Sizes
Crib: 27" x 52"
Twin: 39" x 75"
Full: 54" x 75"
Queen: 60" x 80"
King: 76" x 80"

Changing the size of a quilt

Any of the quilts in this book can easily be made larger or smaller by adding or subtracting blocks.

Charts are given that tell you how many blocks you need to make quilts for each of the mattress sizes listed. Measure your bed and see what kind of a drop you want, then add or subtract blocks accordingly. This is done by dividing the block repeat (6", 9" or 12") into the width and length you want your quilt to be.

This will give you the number of blocks needed for width and length. If the quilt has sashing or borders, plan them into your measurements.

THE BASKET TRELLIS QUILT

The yardage charts list each section of the quilt separately. You may combine yardage from a border and one of the interior fabrics or make up some other combination. The yardage calculations given are generous. This chart is based on a 6" block, a 2¼" sashing, and 6" of border.

	CRIB	TWIN	FULL	QUEEN	KING
Finished Quilt Size	42½ X 55	64 X 80½	74¾ X 80½	85½ X 89	96¼ X 97½
Total blocks	15	40	48	63	80
Vertical sashing strips	2	4	5	6	7
Setting triangles	24	70	84	112	144
Corner triangles	12	20	24	28	32

YARDAGE NEEDED

	CRIB	TWIN	FULL	QUEEN	KING
Basket	¾	1½	1½	1¾	2
Basket background	1	1½	1¾	2⅜	2⅝
Sashing & 1st border					
lengthwise grain	1⅓	2¼	2¼	2¼	2⅝
crosswise grain	½	1	1	1⅓	1⅝
Setting & corner triangles	¾	1⅔	2	2¼	2¾
2nd border	1	1¼	1¼	1¼	1½
Binding	¼	⅜	½	½	½
Backing	2	4	4½	6	9
Batting	47 x 59	68 x 85	79 x 85	90 x 93	100 x 112

When the quilt is wider than the two widths (84"), it will be necessary to purchase an additional length, or you won't have enough backing fabric. The extra fabric could be used in the piecing.

CUTTING GUIDE
Refer to the cutting guide on page 8 to cut the Basket blocks.

	CRIB	TWIN	FULL	QUEEN	KING
Setting triangles: 9¾" x 44" strip	2	5	6	7	9
Corner triangles: 5⅛" x 44" strip	1	2	2	2	2
Vertical sashing: 2¾" x 44" strip					
lengthwise grain (see page 6)	2	4	5	6	7
crosswise grain	3	7	9	11	15
1st border: lengthwise grain: cut two strips for sides (s) 1½" wide and two strips for top/bottom (t/b) 1½" wide					
	33¼" (t/b)	54¾" (t/b)	65½" (t/b)	76¼" (t/b)	87" (t/b)
	45¾" (s)	71¼" (s)	71¼" (s)	79¾" (s)	88¼" (s)
crosswise grain: 1½" x 44" strip	4	6	7	8	9
2nd border: 5½" x 44" strip	5	7	7	8	9
Binding: 1¾" x 44" strip	5	7	8	9	10

BASIC CONSTRUCTION TECHNIQUES

CUTTING

All cutting instructions are given for the use of the rotary cutter. When using the rotary cutter, strips are cut, then they are cut into squares, triangles, and rectangles. When you are using a mat, rotary cutter, and ruler, always place your cutting board on a table and stand over it while you cut. It will be more comfortable and you will be able to exert consistent pressure on the rotary cutter.

If you prefer to cut with scissors, you will need to trace the patterns in the back of the book onto template plastic. You can buy this at your local fabric store or quilt shop. Cut out the template shape. Then trace around the shape onto the back of the fabric and use scissors to cut it out. For the long strips needed in borders and binding, use a yardstick to measure and mark.

MAKING A STRAIGHT-EDGE CUT

Fabric has several properties that you must be conscious of while quiltmaking. The selvage edges are tightly woven and run parallel to the lengthwise or straight of grain. The lengthwise threads are strong and have very little give to them. The crosswise grain runs from selvage to selvage. These threads are more flexible when you pull them. The bias runs at a 45° angle across the crosswise and lengthwise grain. It has the most give. Binding that needs to curve would be cut on the bias.

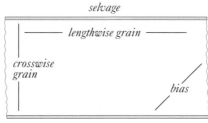

All instructions are given for right-handed people. If you are left-handed, just reverse the instructions.

1. Fold the fabric from selvage to selvage.

Align the straight of the grain the best you can. Bring the center fold of the fabric to the selvages and align it. You will have four layers.

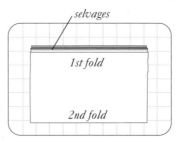

2. Align the 6" side of the ruler with the fold and the selvages. Move the ruler as far as you can to the right and still have four layers of fabric under it. Depress the safety latch on the rotary cutter. Place the fingers of your left hand on the ruler, away from the edge of the ruler. Make a cut starting at the bottom edge and move toward and through the selvages. Press the cutter firmly but not too heavily as you cut.

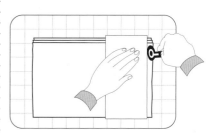

Put the safety back on the blade after every cut. You now have a straight edge to begin your strip cutting. You will follow this procedure on each piece of new fabric that you cut.

3. Lift up the four layers of fabric and turn them so they are on the left-hand side of your board (or walk around the table if you can). The new strip you are cutting needs to be on the left-hand side of the mat.

CUTTING STRIPS

Suppose that you need a 4½" x 44" strip.

1. Align the 4½" mark on the ruler at the left edge of the fabric, with the top edge of the ruler on the selvages. Make a cut by placing the rotary cutter at the bottom of the fabric and moving up to the top edge. Hold the cutter firmly and press with a consistently firm but not hard motion.

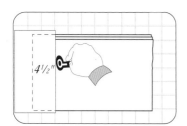

CUTTING SQUARES

Open up the strip of fabric that you just cut. You may stack four rows of strips if you wish. Trim off the selvages.

To cut a 4½" square, align the top edge of the ruler against the top of the fabric. Align the 4½" mark on the ruler with the left edge of the fabric. Make a cut.

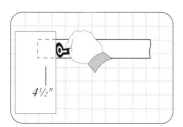

CUTTING THE HALF-SQUARE TRIANGLES

Leave the squares stacked. Place the ruler diagonally across the block, matching the edge of the ruler with both corners. Make a cut.

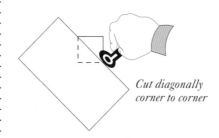

Cut diagonally corner to corner

CUTTING THE QUARTER-SQUARE TRIANGLES

Leave the half-square triangles in place. Lay the ruler across the block to opposite corners and make a cut.

Make a second cut in the opposite direction

SEWING TECHNIQUES

A ¼" seam allowance is ALWAYS used in piecing unless otherwise indicated. It is the most manageable size where several seams meet, and in patchwork there are lots of seams! If you are even a couple of threads off, the problems add up: the block will be too large or too small. It is extremely worthwhile to check your ¼" seam allowance and be accurate from the very beginning.

To check your ¼" seam allowance, draw a line on a piece of paper ¼" away from the cut edge. Place the paper under the presser foot of the sewing machine, with the seam allowance to the right, and bring the needle down through the line that you drew. Release the presser foot. Where the edge of the paper hits on the right is the ¼" distance. If it isn't on the edge of your presser foot, then mark the line with a piece of masking tape on your sewing machine. This tape edge will act as your seam gauge to ensure an accurate ¼" seam.

The stitch length should be set at about 14 to 16 stitches to the inch. The stitch has to be wide enough so you can insert your seam ripper. (Of course you won't be doing any ripping.) No back tacking is necessary.

PRESSING

Pressing is very important in any sewing project. In patchwork, the rule is to press both seam allowances toward the darker fabric whenever possible. Where two seams meet, position them so they go in opposite directions. The two seams will nest together when stitched and the points will match. This may mean that one seam isn't pressed toward the darker fabric. The nesting rule applies first.

Use a dry iron when pressing. Press in an up-and-down motion so that the pieces don't become distorted. Press often.

CHAINING

Whenever you are constructing several blocks, save yourself time by feeding several pairs of fabric pieces through the machine in sequence. To do this, feed the two fabrics through the machine one after the other, without lifting the presser foot. Stitch pairs together along the longer side. There will be a chain of stitches between each pair. Clip the thread between the pieces when finished.

MAKING THE BASKET BLOCK

This simple basket block has a pieced handle which eliminates having to appliqué. The quilts and pillows use various sizes of blocks from 6" to 12". In the quilts pictured, one fabric has been used for the basket and a second for the background. You can also make the stand and the handle a different color from the basket.

Lay the block pieces out on a flat surface next to where you are going to sew, then follow the instructions below:

1. Sew F to E, pressing seam toward F. Sew G to the other side of E/F, pressing seam toward G.

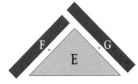

Trim F and G even with E.

2. Sew A to E/F/G, pressing seam toward A. Trim excess seam allowance even with the block.

3. Sew B to D for the left and right sides of the basket. These will be mirror images of each other. Press seam toward D.

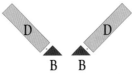

4. Follow the figure below and add H to the basket, then I, then B/D on each side. Press seam toward H/I and B/D. Sew C to unit, pressing seam toward C.

Stitching the Blocks Together

DIAGONAL SET

A diagonal set means that the blocks are arranged at a 45-degree angle (on point) and the seams for the rows are diagonal across the quilt. Setting triangles fill in around the edges with corner triangles finishing the corners. Always lay out the blocks before you begin.

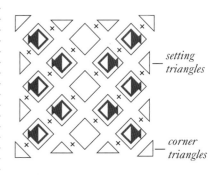

setting triangles

corner triangles

ADDING BORDERS

Borders can act as a frame for quilts as shown by the quilts in this book. The *Old-Fashioned Baskets* quilt has three borders with the first two being stronger colors and narrower than the final floral border. The pillows will give you more border ideas that are adaptable to quilts.

To attach a border strip, start at the sides of the quilt. Lay the right side of the border strip on the right side of the quilt and pin the two layers in place. With the back facing you, stitch ¼" from the edge. Press both seam allowances toward the border. Repeat on the other side of the quilt. Add the top and bottom borders in the same way.

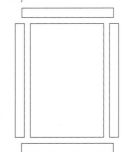

	6"	9"	12"
A: cut the square, then cut diagonally.	4⅞"	6⅞"	8⅞"
B: cut the square, then cut diagonally.	1⅞"	2⅜"	2⅞"
C: cut the square, then cut diagonally.	2⅞"	3⅞"	4⅞"
D: cut 2	1½" x 4½"	2" x 6½"	2½" x 8½"
E: cut the square, then cut diagonally.	3⅞"	5⅜"	6⅞"
F: cut 1	1" x 4¾"	1¼" x 6½"	1½" x 8¼"
G: cut 1	1" x 5½"	1¼" x 7¼"	1½" x 9¼"
H: cut 1	1½" x 4½"	2" x 6½"	2½" x 8½"
I: cut 1	1½" x 5½"	2" x 8"	2½" x 10½

PILLOWS

From Basket blocks, you can construct three different styles of pillows. One is a Medallion Basket *embellished with ribbons and buttons, the next is a* Four Basket, *and the third is a* Single Basket. *The* Four Basket *design is also adaptable for a quilt. The* Medallion Basket *and* Four Basket *pillows fit perfectly over purchased pillow forms, but the smaller* Single Basket *pillow needs to be stuffed with fiberfill.*

Medallion Pillow

YARDAGE NEEDED

The finished size is 18" x 18". The block size is 9".

 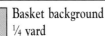

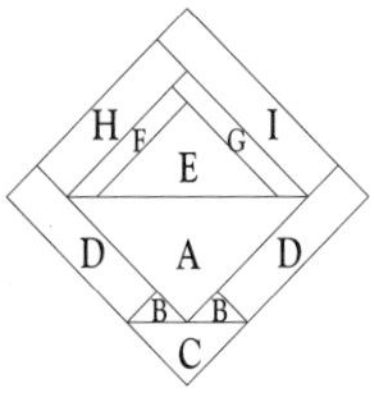

You'll need 2⅛ yards of ¾"-wide ribbon, 10 to 15 assorted ¾"-wide buttons, 6 to 8 ribbon roses, and a 18" pillow form or 12 oz. of fiberfill to complete the pillow.

Basket ¼ yard	**A:** cut a 6⅞" square, then cut the square in half diagonally. **B:** cut a 2⅜" square, then cut the square in half diagonally. **F:** cut a 1¼" x 6½" rectangle. **G:** cut a 1¼" x 7¼" rectangle.	
Basket background ¼ yard	**C:** cut a 3⅞" square, then cut the square in half diagonally. **D:** cut two 2" x 6½" rectangles. **E:** cut a 5⅜" square, then cut the square in half diagonally. **H:** cut a 2" x 6½" rectangle. **I:** cut a 2" x 8" rectangle.	
Corner triangles ¼ yard	Cut two 7" squares, then cut the squares in half diagonally.	
Border and backing ¾ yard	**Border:** Cut two 3½" x 13" strips for the side border. Cut two 3½" x 18½" strips for the top and bottom border. **Backing:** Cut two 11½" x 18½" rectangles, when using a pillow form. Cut one 18½" square when using fiberfill.	

SEWING INSTRUCTIONS

Read the sewing instructions before you begin.

1. Follow the block construction instructions on page 8 to make one basket block.

2. Add two corner triangles to opposite sides of the block, pressing toward the triangles.

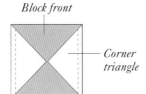

Block front

Corner triangle

Repeat for remaining triangles.

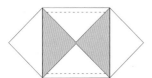

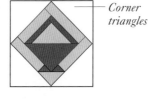

Corner triangles

3. Follow the Adding Borders instructions on page 8 to complete the first border.

4. Place the ribbon at the edge of the border and stitch along both edges. Overlap ribbons at the corners. Refer to the photograph for button and ribbon rose placement. When attaching the buttons, double the thread and sew through the button hole twice. Knot the thread on the back.

5. With right sides facing, place pillow front and back together. Using ¼" seam allowance, sew edges closed, leaving a 5" opening. Turn right side out and press. Fill with tiny wads of fiberfill or use a pillow form. Turn the raw edges under ¼" and slip-stitch opening closed.

Option: For a two-piece backing, press one 18½" edge under ¼". Turn the edge under ¼" again, and stitch close to the edge. Repeat for the remaining rectangle. To create an 18½" square backing, overlap the stitched edges 3½". This overlap creates an opening for the pillow form after the backing is stitched to the front. See Step 5 to finish the pillow, omitting the opening.

Four Basket Pillow and Single Basket Pillow

YARDAGE NEEDED

The block size is 6" for both pillows.

The Four Basket pillow's finished size is 16" x 16". It requires a 16" pillow form or 12 oz. of fiberfill. Baskets: If using four different fabrics, stack the basket fabric when cutting.

The Single Basket pillow's finished size is 10" x 10". It requires 1⅓ yards of ⅜"-wide ribbon, 1⅓ yards of ⅝"-wide flat lace, four medium roses, and 10 oz. of fiberfill.

Four Basket 6" x 16" piece of four different fabrics **Single Basket** 6" x 16" piece of one fabric	**A:** cut a 4⅞" square, then cut in half diagonally. **B:** cut a 1⅞" square, then cut in half diagonally. **F:** cut a 1" x 4¾" rectangle. **G:** cut a 1" x 5½" rectangle.
Four Basket background ⅓ yard **Single Basket background** ⅛ yard	**C:** cut a 2⅞" square, then cut in half diagonally. **D:** cut two 1½" x 4½" rectangles. **E:** cut a 3⅞" square, then cut in half diagonally. **H:** cut a 1½" x 4½" rectangle. **I:** cut a 1½" x 5½" rectangle.
Four Basket corner posts ⅛ yard	Cut four 2½" squares.
Four Basket border and backing ½ yard	**Border:** Cut four 2½" x 12½" rectangles. **Backing:** Cut two 16½" x 10½" pieces or cut one 16½" square when using fiberfill.
Single Basket border and backing ⅓ yard	**Border:** Cut two 2½" x 6½" rectangles for the side borders. Cut two 2½" x 10½" rectangles for the top and bottom borders. **Backing:** Cut one 10½" x 10½" square.

SEWING INSTRUCTIONS

Read the sewing instructions before you begin.

FOUR BASKET PILLOW

1. Follow the block construction directions on page 8 to make four blocks. Referring to the photograph for placement, sew the Basket blocks together.

2. Sew one border strip to each side of the Four Basket block. Sew a corner post to each end of the remaining border strips, then sew strips to top and bottom of pillow.

3. Follow the instructions on page 10, Step 5, for finishing the pillow.

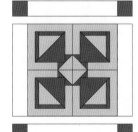

SINGLE BASKET PILLOW

1. Follow the block construction instructions on page 8 to make a Basket block.

2. Follow the Adding Borders instructions on page 8 to complete the border.

3. Place ribbon at the inside edge of the borders and stitch on both sides of the ribbon. Overlap ribbons at the inner corners. Hand stitch roses atop ribbon intersections at inner corners, referring to the photograph on page 9.

4. Follow the instructions on page 10, Step 5, for finishing the pillow.

5. Slip-stitch lace to pillow edges, easing it around the corners.

BASKET TRELLIS

A variety of black floral prints form the baskets in this Victorian-style quilt. The soft, raspberry pink floral background is a larger print, and when cut apart it will change its look. The striped black and cream ticking for the sashing and borders is a good contrast in fabric style to all of the florals.

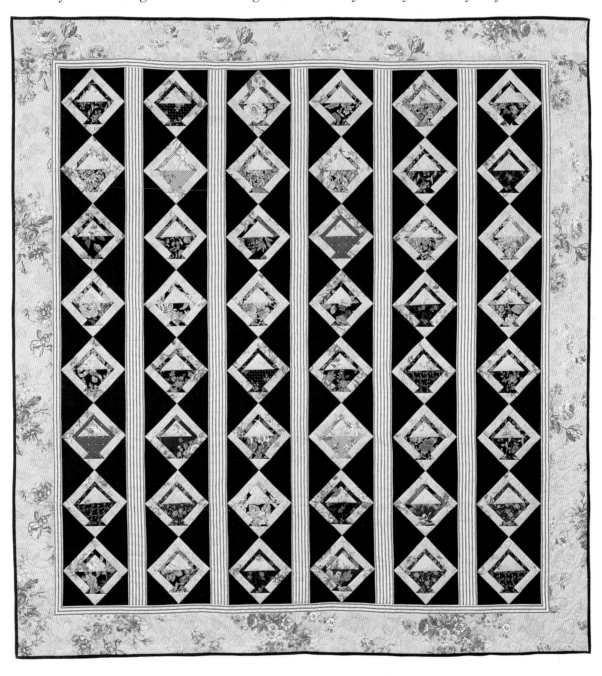

YARDAGE NEEDED

The finished size is 74¾" x 80½". The block size is 6".

Baskets: *Instructions are given for cutting single baskets since this is a scrap basket quilt using many fabrics. Stack the fabrics four deep, right sides up, to streamline cutting. If you want to use the fabric a second time, put it in another stack. You will need a total of 48 baskets.*

Basket background: *Instructions given are for streamline cutting the 48 backgrounds.*

Baskets
8 to 10 fabrics totaling
1½ yards

A: cut a 4⅞" square, then cut the square in half diagonally. This gives you two basket bodies.
B: cut a 1⅞" square, then cut the square in half diagonally.
F: cut a 1" x 4¾" rectangle.
G: cut a 1" x 5½" rectangle.

Basket background
and 2nd border
2¾ yards

C: cut two 2⅞" x 44" strips, then cut the strips into twenty-four squares.
Cut the squares in half diagonally.
D: cut eleven 1½" x 44" strips, then cut the strips into ninety-six 4½" rectangles.
E: cut three 3⅞" x 44" strips, then cut the strips into twenty-four squares.
Cut the squares in half diagonally.
H: cut six 1½" x 44" strips, then cut the strips into forty-eight 4½" rectangles.
I: cut seven 1½" x 44" strips, then cut the strips into forty-eight 5½" rectangles.
2nd border: Cut seven 5½" x 44" strips. Piece together the strips into one long strip, then cut two strips to 70½" for the sides. Then cut two strips to 74¾" for the top and bottom.

Sashing and 1st border
2¼ yards

1st border: Cut on lengthwise grain. Cut two 1½" x 71½" strips for the sides.
Cut two 1½" x 65½" strips for the top and bottom.
Sashing: Cut on lengthwise grain. Cut five 2¾" x 68½" strips.

Setting and corner triangles
and binding
2½ yards

Setting triangles: 84 total. Cut five 9¾" x 44" strips, then cut the strips into twenty 9¾" squares. Cut one more 9¾" square, then cut all twenty-one squares into quarter-square triangles.
Corner triangles: 24 total. Cut two 5⅛" x 44" strips, then cut the strips into twelve 5⅛" squares. Cut the squares in half diagonally.
Binding: Cut eight 1¾" x 44" strips. Piece together two strips for each side, then cut the strips to 80½". Repeat piecing the strips for the top and bottom, then cut strips to 74¾".

Backing 4½ yards
Batting 79" x 85"

Cut two 44" x 2¼ yards lengths for the backing. Trim off the selvages and sew sections together, right sides facing, along the lengthwise grain.

SEWING INSTRUCTIONS

Read the sewing instructions before you begin.

1. Follow the block construction instructions on page 8 to make 48 blocks.

2. Arrange eight blocks vertically in a row, inserting side and corner triangles. Sew together diagonally as shown on page 8. Complete six vertical rows.

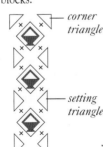

corner triangle

setting triangle

3. Sew a sashing strip between each row.

4. For the first border, use the patterns on page 22 to cut a 45° angle at each end of the strips.

trim *trim*
Borders will look like this.

5. With a pencil, mark the dots from the patterns onto the wrong side of the border strips.

6. With right sides together, place the border strips atop the quilt top. Position the border strip dots ¼" in from the corner and pin.

7. Sew one side of the border to the quilt at a time; sew from the dot to the dot and STOP; back tack one stitch at the beginning and the end. When you add the next border to

the quilt, the dots will match up in the corner. Always sew to the dot and STOP.

8. To join the mitered corner, place the two corners together and sew from the dot to the outer edge. Press open.

Stitch from dot to outer corner.

Press seam to open.

9. Follow the Adding Borders instructions on page 8 to complete the second border.

10. Follow the general instructions starting on page 20 for finishing the quilt.

LANCASTER MEDALLION

A single bright-colored basket against a black background forms the center of this quilt. The second color comes into play in the smaller baskets and the border. Machine quilting fills the background spaces to complete this Amish-inspired quilt.

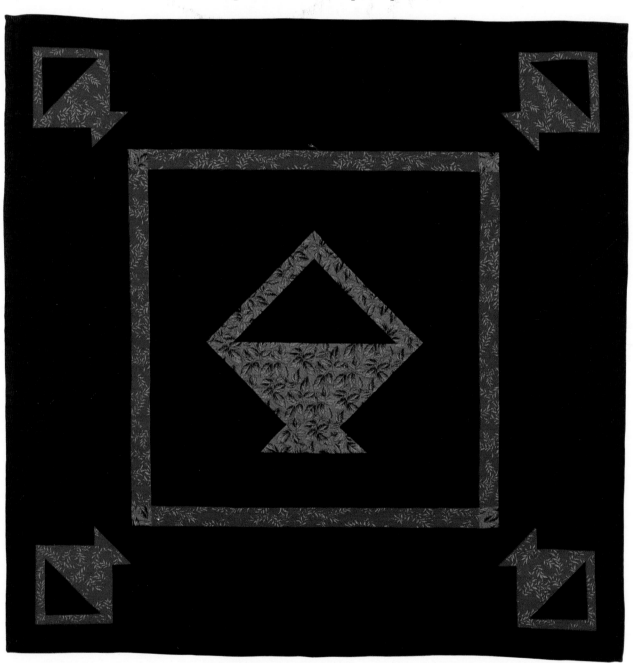

YARDAGE NEEDED

The finished size is 31½" x 31½". The block sizes are 6" and 12".

■	**12" Basket and corner posts** ¼ yard	**A:** cut one 8⅞" square, then cut in half diagonally. **B:** cut one 2⅞" square, then cut in half diagonally. **F:** cut one 1½" x 8¼" rectangle. **G:** cut one 1½" x 9¼" rectangle. **Corner Posts:** Cut four 1½" squares.
■	**6" Baskets and 1st border** ¼ yard	**A:** cut two 4⅞" squares, then cut in half diagonally. **B:** cut four 1⅞" squares, then cut in half diagonally. **F:** cut four 1" x 4¾" rectangles. **G:** cut four 1" x 5½" rectangles. **1st border:** Cut four 1½" x 17½" strips.
■	**Basket background,** **corner triangles, 2nd border,** **and binding** 1⅛ yards	**12" Basket background fabric:** **C:** cut one 4⅞" square, then cut in half diagonally. **D:** cut two 2½" x 8½" rectangles. **E:** cut one 6⅞" square, then cut in half diagonally. **H:** cut one 2½" x 8½" rectangle. **I:** cut one 2½" x 10½" rectangle. **6" Basket background fabric:** **C:** cut two 2⅞" squares, then cut in half diagonally. **D:** cut eight 1½' x 4½" rectangles. **E:** cut two 3⅞" squares, then cut in half diagonally. **H:** cut four 1½" x 4½" rectangles. **I:** cut four 1½" x 5½" rectangles. **Corner Triangles:** Cut two 9⅜" squares, then cut in half diagonally. **2nd border:** Cut four 6½" x 19½" strips. **Binding:** Cut two 1¾" x 31½" strips for the sides. Cut two 1¾" x 32" strips for the top and bottom.
	Backing 1 yard **Batting 33" x 33"**	Cut one 36" x 36" piece.

SEWING INSTRUCTIONS

Read the sewing instructions before you begin.

1. Follow the block construction instructions on page 8 to make one 12" block for the center and four 6" blocks for the borders.

2. Attach the corner triangles to the 12" center block.

Block front

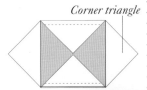
Corner triangle

Corner triangle

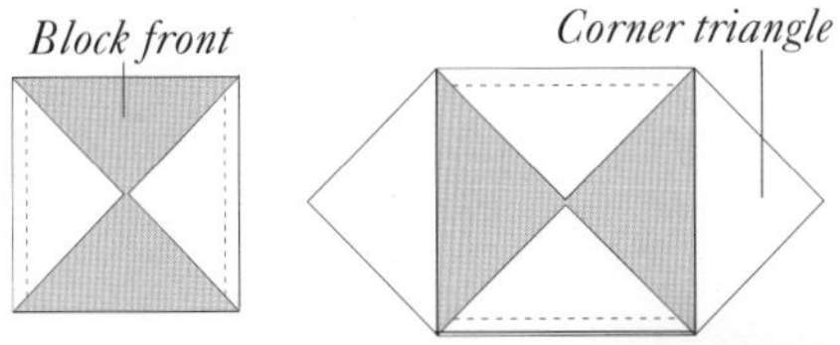

3. Sew one border strip to each side of the center block. Sew a corner post to each end of the remaining border strips, then sew strips to top and bottom of center block.

4. Follow the same procedure for adding the second border.

5. Follow the general instructions starting on page 20 for finishing the quilt.

OLD-FASHIONED BASKETS

Several years ago I saw a quilt in a museum that had baskets set on their sides facing each other. The fabrics I chose for this quilt have an 1800s feeling to them. I wanted to capture the feeling with the fabrics and setting in this quilt. Finding colored fabrics with a "mellow mood" and setting them on a deep tan background re-created the feeling and look of the antique quilt.

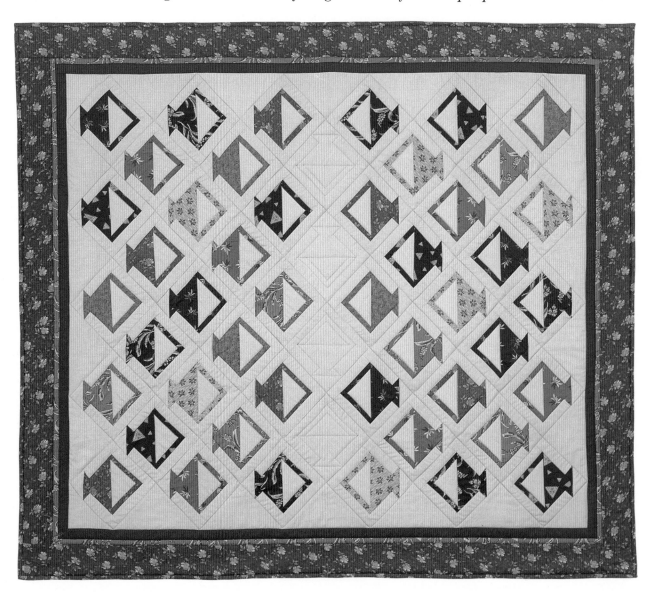

YARDAGE NEEDED

The finished size is 52" x 60½". The block size 6".

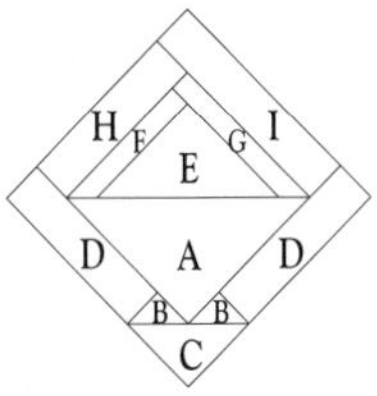

Baskets: *Instructions are given for cutting single baskets since this is a scrap basket quilt using many fabrics. Stack the fabrics four deep, right sides up, to streamline cutting. If you want to use the fabric a second time, put it in another stack. You will need a total of 46 baskets.*
Basket background: *Instructions given are for streamline cutting the 46 backgrounds.*

Baskets 1½ yards total of 6 to 8 fabrics	**A:** cut a 4⅞" square, then cut in half diagonally (this gives you two basket bodies). **B:** cut a 1⅞" square, then cut in half diagonally. **F:** cut a 1" x 4¾" rectangle. **G:** cut a 1" x 5½" rectangle.

Basket background, center squares, setting triangles, and corner triangles   2⅓ yards

Background:
C: cut two 2⅞" x 44" strips, then cut into twenty-three squares.
Cut squares in half diagonally.
D: cut eleven 1½" x 44" strips, then cut the strips into ninety-two 4½" rectangles.
E: cut three 3⅞" x 44" strips, then cut the strips into twenty-three squares.
Cut the squares in half diagonally.
H: cut six 1½" x 44" strips, then cut the strips into forty-six 4½" rectangles.
I: cut six 1½" x 44" strips, then cut the strips into forty-six 5½" rectangles.
Center squares: Cut one 6½" x 27" strip, then cut the strip into four squares.
Setting Triangles: 18 total. Cut one 9¾" x 44" strip, then cut the strip into four squares.
Cut one more square to total five, then cut all the squares into quarter-square triangles.
Corner Triangles: 4 total. Cut two 5⅛" squares, then cut in half diagonally.

1st border ¼ yard	Cut five 1½" x 44" strips. Piece together the strips into one long strip. Cut two strips 43" for the sides. Cut two strips 53½" for the top and bottom.
2nd border ¼ yard	Cut five 1" x 44" strips. Piece together the strips into one long strip. Cut two strips 45" for the sides. For the top and bottom, cut two strips 54½".
3rd border, backing, and binding 4¼ yards	**3rd Border:** Cut five 3½" x 44" strips and one 3½" x 5". Piece together the strips into one long strip. For each side, cut the strips to 46". For the top and bottom, cut the strips to 60½". **Backing:** Cut two 44" x 56" rectangles. Trim off the selvages and sew together along the lengthwise grain. Trim to 56" x 64½". **Binding:** Cut five 1¾" x 44" strips and one 1¾" x 16". Piece together the strips into one lengthwise strip, then cut two strips 52" for the sides. Cut two strips 61" for the top and bottom.

Batting 56" x 64½"

SEWING INSTRUCTIONS

Read the sewing instructions before you begin.

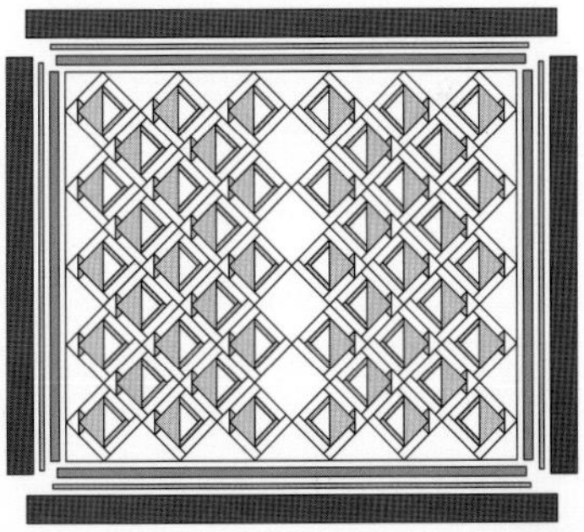

1. Follow the block construction instructions on page 8 to make 46 blocks.

2. Refer to the photograph for block layout, inserting the setting triangles and corners. Follow the instructions on page 8 for a diagonal setting.

3. Follow the Adding Borders instructions on page 8 to complete the borders.

4. Follow the general instructions starting on page 20 for finishing the quilt.

WINDOW BOX BASKETS

This is a small wall quilt that might adorn a kitchen wall. Two versions are presented: summer baskets with sky blue fabric and bright floral baskets, and a winter quilt with tiny chickadees on a woodsy background, plus red and black checkered baskets. You may have more ideas for different palettes to use in this simple quilt.

Summer

Winter

YARDAGE NEEDED

The finished size is 13" x 45". The block size is 6".

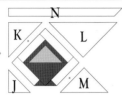

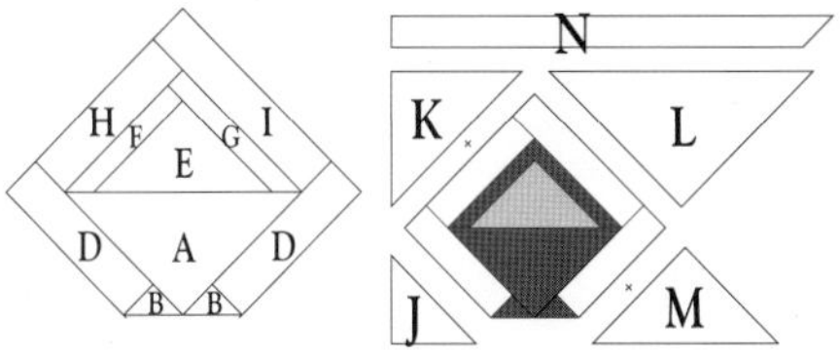

Icons correspond to the colors in the winter quilt.

Baskets ¼ yard	**A:** cut a 4⅞" square, then cut in half diagonally (this gives you two baskets). **B:** cut a 1⅞" square, then cut in half diagonally. **F:** cut a 1" x 4¾" rectangle. **G:** cut a 1" x 5½" rectangle.
Border and binding ½ yard	**Border:** Cut three 1½" x 44" strips. Piece together the strips into one long strip. Cut two 1½" x 11" strips for the sides. Cut two 1½" x 44½" strips for the top and bottom. **Binding:** Cut three 1¾" x 44" strips. Piece together the strips in one long strip, then cut two strips 12¾" for the sides. For the top and bottom, cut two strips 45½".
Basket background, setting and corner triangles, and backing 1 yard	**Basket background:** **D:** cut two 1½" x 4½" rectangles. **E:** cut a 3⅞" square, then cut in half diagonally (this gives you two backgrounds). **H:** cut a 1½" x 4½" rectangle. **I:** cut a 1½" x 5½" rectangle. **Setting triangles:** **L:** cut one 9¾" square, then cut into quarter-square triangles. **M:** cut one 7" square, then cut into quarter-square triangles. **Corner triangles:** **K:** cut a 5⅛" square, then cut in half diagonally. **J:** cut a 3¾" square, then cut in half diagonally. **N:** cut a 1¾" x 43½" strip (you may need to piece this if your fabric isn't wide enough). **Backing:** Cut and piece a 17" x 49" rectangle.
Light check ⅛ yard	Cut two 1½" x 44" strips each of the light and dark fabric.
Dark check ⅛ yard	

Batting 17" x 49"

SEWING INSTRUCTIONS

Read the sewing instructions before you begin.

1. Follow the block construction instructions on page 8 to make five blocks, eliminating C from the corner of the blocks.

2. Following the quilt photograph, lay out setting triangles and corner triangles. Sew together diagonally as shown on page 8. Add N to the top of the quilt.

3. To make the checkerboard, stitch strips together alternating colors as shown. Cut across the strips at 1½" intervals. Stitch these together until you have two rows of 43 squares. You may have to take one square off and add it to the other end on one of the strips. Mark the centers of the checkerboard border and the center basket; pin together and sew to the bottom of the quilt. If necessary, trim excess checkerboard border at edges.

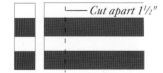

— Cut apart 1½"

4. Follow the Adding Borders instructions on page 8 to complete the border.

5. Follow the general instructions starting on page 20 for finishing the quilt.

FINISHING THE QUILT

Marking the quilt

If you need to mark any quilt designs before quilting, check the washability of your pencil on a scrap of fabric first. Heat will set most pencil marks, so do not press the fabric after marking. If the fabrics have not been pre-washed, sometimes the pencil marks will not wash out. There are fabric erasers, available in notions sections of fabric and quilt shops, which will remove most pencil marks. Check the washability. Your gridded ruler is convenient for marking straight quilting lines. If any marking for quilting is necessary, do the marking before you layer the quilt. Quarter-inch masking tape is available at fabric stores and quilt shops. Use it to mark stitching lines. (Stitch beside the edge of the tape.) Then remove the tape and reuse it. There are also numerous stencils available with quilting motifs at your local stores. Some you trace around, others are paper that can be stitched through and torn away.

Layering the quilt

Prepare the backing by sewing any seams to make a piece large enough for the quilt (see individual quilt instructions). We have planned the batting and backing to be at least one inch or more larger than the finished size all around. The extra will be trimmed off later.

Bed sheets can be used for quilt backing in some cases: since they have a high thread count, they are difficult to hand quilt, but they can be quilted easily by machine. Flannel is a good backing for baby and juvenile quilts, since the nap makes it stick to the bed.

Layering and basting needs to be done on a hard surface, either a large table or the floor.

1. Place the backing wrong side up on the surface. Use the ⅝"-wide masking tape and tape each corner to the surface, making sure the fabric is taut. Then tape the centers of each side and work toward the corners. Tape about every 12".

taping the quilt back

2. Place the batting on the backing. Do not stretch or distort it, but it may need straightening and patting down.

3. Lay the quilt top right side up onto the batting, centering it on the batting and backing. Smooth it out.

4. Basting may be done with safety pins or thread. Both methods are given. To safety-pin baste, start at the center and pin about every 8" to 10". To baste with a thread, use a large embroidery needle and a single thread knotted at the end. Follow the figure below and start from the center, taking large stitches to the sides. Knot the thread at the end. Go back to the center each time.

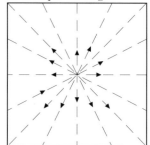

quilt basting

Quilting

Directions will be given for machine and hand quilting. Either method will work. Most of our quilts are machine-quilted, since it is faster. Always do a practice test on layered fabric if you are machine quilting to make sure your machine is in good working order.

Quilting by Machine

If your machine has a walking foot or even-feed foot, you will find machine quilting much easier. There are three layers to be fed under the foot and the top layer can easily drag. The walking foot feeds all three layers evenly through the machine.

Machine-quilted quilts in this book are stitched in the ditch. This means that no marking is necessary, because the stitching follows the seam lines. Most quilts are first stitched "in the ditch." This means stitching as close to the seam as possible

stitch close to seam

Use this method to stitch around blocks and borders. Then decorative quilting can be done in the other spaces. Any specific quilting instructions appear with the individual quilt directions. Remove the basting or pins as you quilt in each area.

1. When machine quilting, put your machine on a large table or place a card table behind your machine. As the quilt feeds through the machine, it can rest on the table instead of pulling. If you are quilting a large quilt, you may find it necessary to roll the side of the quilt that goes under the arm of the machine.

2. Put monofilament thread in the top of your machine and regular thread in the bobbin to match the back of the quilt.

3. At the beginning and end of each line of stitching, secure the threads by back-tacking two stitches. Clip threads as you finish each seam.

4. Line up the quilt so it can feed straight through the machine. Spread the seam with your fingers as you stitch, and stitch a little to the side of the seam, away from the seam allowance. When you move your hands, the fabric relaxes and hides the stitching. When all the quilting is finished, remove the basting stitches.

Hand quilting

Hand quilting is done with a shorter, sharp needle. Needles start at size 8, the largest needle, and go to a 12. The finer the needle and the thinner the batting, the smaller the stitch. The consistency of the size of the stitches is more important than having tiny stitches. The thickness of the batting helps to determine whether the stitches are small or not. As you practice and do more quilting, your stitches will become smaller and more consistent.

Hand quilting was done traditionally ¼" from the seam lines. Then some of the larger spaces would have a design quilted in them. To find stencils for quilting designs, visit your local quilt shop. Use the ¼" masking tape along the edge of the seam as a guide for hand quilting. It is reusable 4 to 5 times.

Most people find it easiest to quilt in a hoop. The three layers are held taut and it is easier to get consistent stitches. Traditionally hoops were round, but you now see the PVC pipe square frames that work well as you near the corners. There is also a half hoop that lets you quilt right up to the edge of the quilt. Large floor frames are still used for large quilts, but many of today's homes simply do not have room to leave a frame set up for any length of time.

1. Use a single thread about 18" long and knotted at one end. To secure the knot under the top layer of the fabric, take a single stitch through the top layer only, toward where you want to begin your quilting. Pull the thread slightly until the knot opens the weave of the fabric and slips through. The knot pops through more easily if you put the needle between two of the fabric threads.

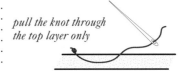

pull the knot through the top layer only

2. The quilting stitch is an up-and-down motion. Insert the needle from the top to the back side, making a stitch an eighth to a tenth of an inch long. As you get the feel of it, you will be able to get several stitches on the needle. I find that it takes me about 15 minutes to get into the rhythm of quilting each time I pick it up.

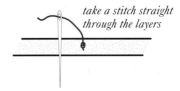

take a stitch straight through the layers

3. When you reach the end of your line of quilting, make a single knot in the thread.

4. Take a small stitch through the top layer only and pull the knot through the opening. Trim off the excess thread and remove the basting.

BINDING

1. Stitch the binding strips together into one long length.

2. Refer to the specific quilt you are making to find out how long to cut the strips for each edge.

3. Place the side binding strip along the edge of the quilt, with right sides together, and sew ¼" away from the edge.

4. Trim off the excess batting and backing to match the ¼" seam allowance.

5. Press the raw edge of the binding under ¼". Fold the binding to the back of the quilt and line up the folded edge of the binding with the seam line you just stitched to attach the binding to the quilt. Pin every few inches.

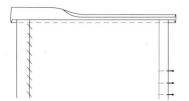

6. Slip stitch the side binding to the back of the quilt.

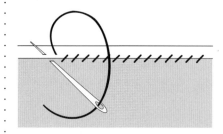

7. Repeat Steps 3–6 for the remaining side, top, and bottom bindings. At the corners, fold under the raw edges of the top and bottom bindings even with the side bindings.

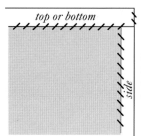

top or bottom

side

tuck under seeam allowance and stitch

¼" seam allowance is included in all patterns.

Border Miter Pattern
Place on left end.

sew this edge first to quilt top.

Border Miter Pattern
Place on right end.

sew this edge first to quilt top.

¼" seam allowance is included in all patterns.

These are the triangles for the 6", 9", and 12" Basket blocks.

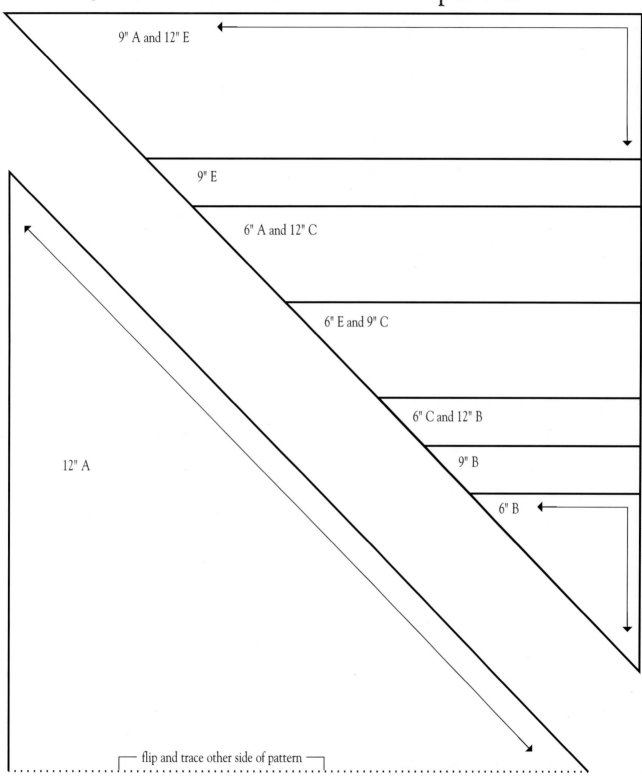

9" A and 12" E

9" E

6" A and 12" C

6" E and 9" C

6" C and 12" B

9" B

6" B

12" A

flip and trace other side of pattern

12" I

12" D and H

9" I

9" D and H

6" I

6" D and H

¼" seam allowance is included in all patterns.

These are the patterns for the 6", 9", and 12" Basket blocks.

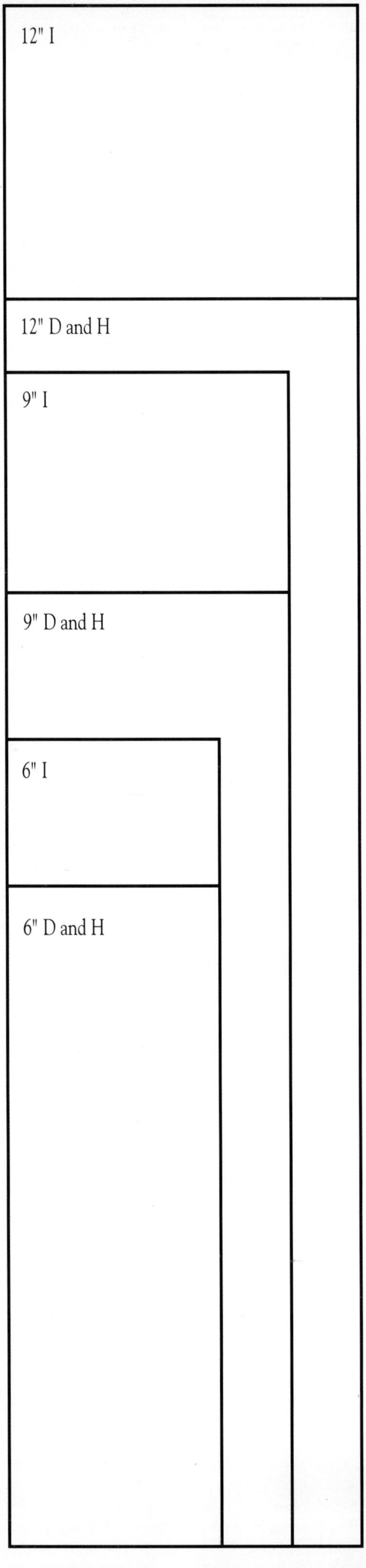

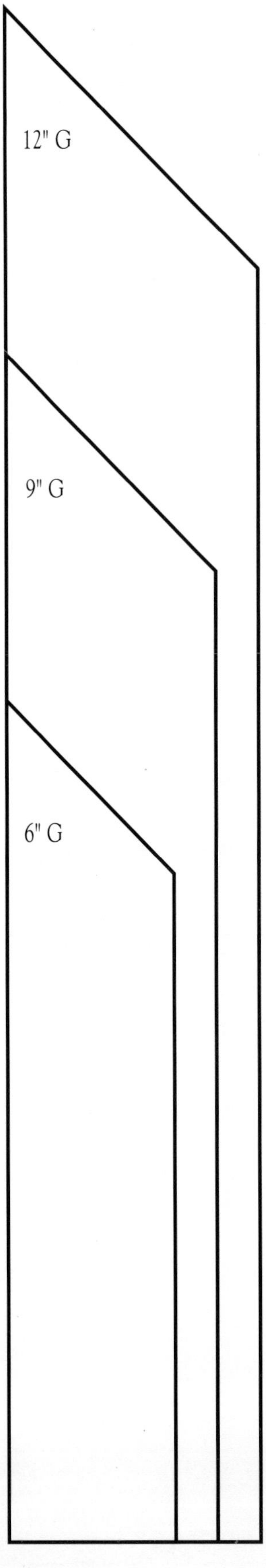

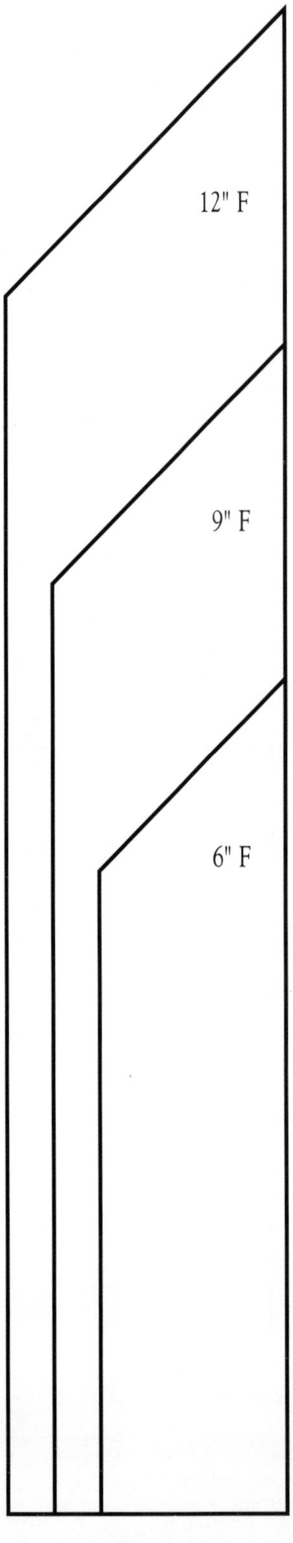

12" G

9" G

6" G

12" F

9" F

6" F